better together*

*This book is best read together, grownup and kid.

a kids book about™ shame

by Jamie Letorneau

a kids book about™

Library of Congress Cataloging-in-Publication Data is available.

This book represents the author's personal experience and thus is not intended to be representative of every form or example of shame as it applies to the many who have experienced it in their lives.

A Kids Book About Shame is available online at: akidsbookabout.com

To share your stories, ask questions, or inquire about bulk purchases (schools, libraries, and non-profits), please use the following email address:

hello@akidsbookabout.com

www.akidsbookabout.com

ISBN: 9781951253295

Printed in the USA

For anyone facing shame, may you feel understood
and loved in the pages of this book.

Intro

Everyone is capable of feeling shame, including kids. Some of us experience it and some of us live in it. But, it doesn't mean we have to carry it by ourselves. Shame is confusing and overwhelming, especially for kids, and they need help navigating it as it can stick around. It can follow us through life like weird little monsters and make us feel like we're not enough. So the more we talk about our shame, the more we can identify it, wrangle it, and live more freely as ourselves.

This book isn't here to tell kids that shame is bad. It's here to tell them that shame is part of being human. And feeling it doesn't make them any less.

Hi.

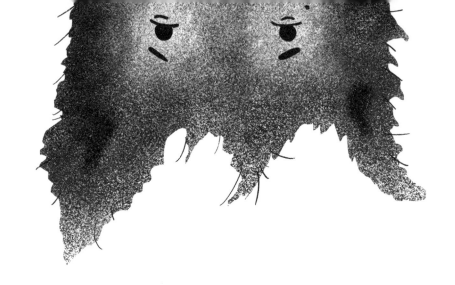

Pssst... this is where you say "Hi."

It's ok, sometimes I get shy, too.

P.S. Did you know we all feel shy sometimes?

Can I tell you something else
most people feel?

Shame.

Have you ever heard
the word, "shame"?

It's something most people feel,
but don't talk about much.

You probably haven't heard of it because that's what we do.

When we feel shame, we try to hide it. And we definitely **don't** talk about it.

It's scary to show anyone
or let them know
what you feel shame about.

Really scary.

So what is shame?

Shame is a tricky **feeling** that
crawls into our brains
and our hearts
that makes us feel icky,
like we're **not enough:**
not nice enough,
brave enough,
happy enough,
smart enough...

just not enough.

Shame **isn't** just doing something wrong—

like failing a math test.

Shame **isn't** just doing something by accident—

like breaking someone's favorite toy.

It's thinking that **YOU** are wrong.

Sometimes we feel shame because of something we did or didn't do.

Other times we feel shame because of something done **to** us.

Other times,
we don't know why we feel shame.

Shame is a thing that **sticks** with you,
and doesn't just go away.

And sometimes,
it never says goodbye.

But shame doesn't always
look or act or feel the same way...

Sometimes shame feels like playing hide-and-seek but not wanting to be found.

Shame feels like
you're dirty and broken
on the inside and outside.

Shame feels like

climbing over a giant pile
of stinky garbage
that never, ever gets smaller.

Shame feels like
an unwanted shadow
that follows you around.

Shame feels like
being around a bunch of people
and still being alone.

Shame feels like not knowing how to make everyone happy or whose version of right & wrong you should follow.

Shame can look like so many different things...

And it can confuse, exhaust, hurt, annoy, scare, and sadden you...

But I want you to know something.

Something very important.

Something **so very, very** important
that I don't want you to forget.

You're not alone.

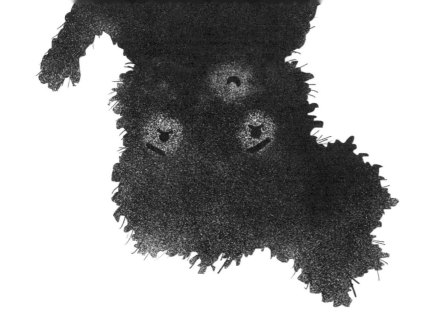

Yup. Moms, dads, siblings, friends, teachers...even your dog sometimes feel shame.

Shame is not a fun thing
to discuss with anyone.

But, it can do **SO** much good
to just talk about it.

To share your feelings.
Your shame.

And when you do that,
you might just find
someone else who needed to talk
about their shame, too.

And maybe, just maybe you'll see...

that you and all of us...

are already enough...

There's no special thing for you
to say or change or do.

You'll see the creature
that follows you
and whispers,
"Shame on you,"
begin to fade away this time,
and start to say **goodbye**.

Go ahead, try to talk,
you can set it free.

If you're not ready to talk it through,
that's ok, and **you're ok**, too.

You can do other things to help.........................

..........................You can **draw.**
You can **write.**
You can **dance.**
You can **jump.**
You can **sing.**
You can **swing.**
You can **do all sorts** of things.

Just.

Get.

It.

Out.

It may not be easy,
    but it may not be hard.

It might not feel good,
    but what if it could?

Maybe you can try—
because you know what?

You are pretty great
and that should be **enough**.

BECAUSE

YOU

ARE
ENOUGH.

good, wonderful, fantastic, strong, beautiful
unstoppable, intelligent, brave, smart, funny
memorable, enthusiastic, encouraging, shining
well, brilliant, outstanding, stupendous, marv
beneficent, thoughtful, empathetic, good-he
bright, luminous, marvelous, ex

You are

honest, patient, generous, war
vely, nurturing, honorable, exciting, dynami
oyful, peaceful, exceptional, willing, reliabl
isionary, inspired, awesome, patient, enjoya
exemplary, first-rate, courteous, gracious, wc
igorous, tolerant, ethical, kindhearted, gen
aluable, crack, select, splendid, ace, reliable
old, gentle, handsome, superb, delightfu
miable, pleasant, magical, centered, cozy, a
mbitious, persistent, aware, wild, selfless, op
andy, attentive, present, explorative, colorfu
boosting, sweet, chipper, silly, soulful, natu
nspiring, festive, contemplative, healing, ep
harp, clever, hip, stimulating, effervescent

kind, creative, fun, fabulous, great, amazin
fast, unique, fab, caring, thoughtful, coc
g, phenomenal, totally rad, admirable, groov
ous, staggering, compassionate, considerat
ted, loving, able, adept, capable, competer
aordinary, courageous, gracious, imaginativ
n, playful, supportive, trustworthy, vibran
curious, charismatic, authentic, empowere
integral, happy, transcendent, original, ap
e, magnificent, fantastic, excellent, distinctiv
ny, perfect, glorious, talented, unrivaled, loya
ne, respectful, complete, interesting, capita
elpful, tolerant, adroit, dependable, meritou
stellar, major, giving, supreme, admirabl
ctionate, comforting, tenacious, determine
n, real, resilient, flexible, diligent, resourcefu
humane, zany, vivacious, relatable, top-notc
, free, endearing, special, adaptive, invitin
, magnanimous, forgiving, unselfish, activ
nerry, intrepid, gallant, spirited, encouragin

However you share,
it doesn't need to be perfect.

Because you are human
and humans aren't perfect.

We have our **different** brains
to think our **different** thoughts.

We have our **different** hearts to
feel our **different** feelings.

So try sharing one way.

And then try another.

And someday
when you're ready,

it won't feel so **heavy**.

Remember, you're enough.

Your **WHOLE** entire self.

Every little bit.

Every.

One.

Matters.

They are enough.

You are enough.

We are
all enough.

Outro

Now that you've helped kids read about shame, how do you help them talk about theirs?

Start with sharing some of your own stories and see if it helps them open up. Here are a few questions you can ask:

> Did you feel shame after you made a mistake?
>
> What does shame feel like to you?
>
> What do you do when you feel shame now?
>
> What can I do to help when you feel shame?

Remember what you would have wanted as a kid. Maybe you wished to be seen and heard for your goodness and not ashamed for whatever you did or did not do that felt so icky. You're not alone and neither are they. Remind yourself. Remind them, too.

find more kids books about

bullying, disabilities, divorce, creativity, racism, empathy, adventure, belonging, failure, money, and anxiety.

akidsbookabout.com

share
your read*

*Tell somebody, post a photo, or give this book away to share what you care about.

@akidsbookabout